Teen

FAQ

Alcohol

Teen
FAQ
Alcohol

Anne Rooney

ARCTURUS

This edition first published in 2010 by Arcturus Publishing
Distributed by Black Rabbit Books
P.O. Box 3263
Mankato
Minnesota MN 56002

Printed in China

Series concept: Discovery Books Ltd.
www.discoverybooks.net
Editors: Amy Bauman and Rachel Minay
Designer: D. R. ink
Consultant: Xanthe Fry, School Counselor and Educational Consultant
Illustrator: Keith Williams
Picture researchers: Tamsin Osler and Rachel Tisdale

Library of Congress Cataloging-in-Publication Data

Rooney, Anne.
   Alcohol / Anne Rooney.
      p. cm. -- (Teen FAQ)
   Includes index.
   ISBN 978-1-84837-702-8 (library binding)
 1. Alcoholism--Juvenile literature. 2. Alcohol--Physiological effect--Juvenile literature. 3. Drinking of alcoholic beverages--Juvenile literature. I. Title.
   HV5066.R66 2011
   613.81--dc22
                                        2010010638

M495

Picture credits
Corbis: cover (S. Hammid), 11 (Mango Productions), 12 (Tomas Rodriguez), 15 (Lance Iversen/San Francisco Chronicle), 21 (Bob Thomas), 23 (Goodshoot), 27 (Jeremy Woodhouse/Blend Images), 28 (Juice Images), 29 (Kevin Dodge), 30 (Richard Hutchings). Getty Images: 16 (Matt Cardy), 19 (Caroline Purser), 26 (Justin Sullivan), 33 (Charlie Schuck), 35 (Kevin Fitzgerald), 42 (Purestock). Istockphoto.com: 7 (Dane Wirtzfeld), 18 (Ryerson Clark), 32 (Jill Chen), 39 (Tyson Paul), 45 left (Jill Chen), 45 right (Ryerson Clark). Photofusion: 6. Science Photo Library: 14 (Arthur Glauberman). Shutterstock: 8 (Jason Stitt), 9 top (iofoto), 9 bottom (Anton Prado PHOTO), 17 (MarFot), 20 (Monkey Business Images), 22, 24, 25 (Alex Hinds), 31 (Christopher Futcher), 34 (Anatema), 37 (iofoto), 38 (Corepics), 40 (prism68), 41 (Lisa F. Young), 43 (Gladskikh Tatiana).

Every attempt has been made to clear copyright. Should there be any inadvertent omission, please apply to the publisher for rectification.

SL001456US
Supplier 03, Date 0510

Contents

1 Is alcohol a problem?

You've probably seen articles on television and in magazines and newspapers about the "alcohol problem," and you may have wondered what the fuss is all about. Why is alcohol suddenly a problem?

Changes in drinking habits

Every generation grumbles that young people are unruly, undisciplined, drink more, and are more badly behaved than their elders ever were—we can even find it in writings of the Romans. But it is true that the health and social problems caused by drinking alcohol have become worse in recent years than they were in the mid-twentieth century.

? WHAT IS ALCOHOL?

Alcohol is a naturally occurring chemical that is produced by the action of yeast on sugar. The chemical process that produces alcohol is called **fermentation**; chemicals from the sugar are converted into a substance that chemists call **ethanol** and most people know as alcohol.

More and more young people are starting to drink alcohol, often below the legal age. It can have an impact on their personal health, their families, and society as a whole.

People of all ages are drinking more now than in the past, and drinks contain more alcohol than they used to. The average American drank 7.8 litres of alcohol in 1960, and this had risen to 8.3 litres by 2000. In the United Kingdom, alcohol consumption doubled in the same period.

Young people—including many who are below the legal age to buy alcohol—are drinking more often and in greater volumes than ever before. This is particularly worrisome, as alcohol is more harmful for young people than for adults.

NOTHING NEW

Alcohol has been used for thousands of years. In the past, in places where there was no clean drinking water, fermented drinks were the safest thing to drink, as alcohol kills germs. People have drunk alcohol as a medicine, as part of religious or magic rituals, and just because they like it.

Does my sister drink too much?

Dear Agony Aunt,
I'm worried about my older sister. She and her college friends go out clubbing most weekends. They drink two or three bottles of wine between four of them, and they have **shots** of vodka as well. Is it bad for her?
Kathryn, 17

Dear Kathryn,
Your sister and her friends are drinking at dangerous levels. The body can't cope well with lots of alcohol in one drinking session, so your sister could be doing real damage to her body. Try suggesting that when she goes out she drinks nonalcoholic cocktails between alcoholic drinks. She should aim to cut her drinking to a safer level (see page 9: Safe drinking limits).

Measuring alcohol

The amount of alcohol in a drink is indicated by a figure on the packaging showing the "abv" or "alcohol by volume." This is the percentage of a drink that is pure alcohol. If a drink is marked as 10 percent abv or 10 percent vol, then in 12 ounces of the drink there are 1.2 ounces of pure alcohol. Some drinks show instead a figure for "proof," which is an older way of measuring alcohol content. Proof is double the abv figure, so a drink that is 40 percent proof is 20 percent alcohol by volume.

Keeping track

To make it easier to keep track, alcohol consumption is measured in "standard drinks" (United States and Australia) or "units" (United Kingdom). It's important to follow country guidelines as they refer to local measures for drinks.

In the United States

1 standard drink = 0.5 oz (13.6 g) of pure alcohol

= 12 oz of beer or cooler

= 5 oz of wine

= 8–9 oz of malt liquor

= 1.5 oz of spirits (hard liquor)

In the United Kingdom

1 unit = 10 ml (8 g) of pure alcohol

= a third of a pint of beer that is 5–6% abv

= half a standard (175 ml) glass of wine that is 12% abv

= a single measure (25 ml) of spirits that is 40% abv

In Australia

1 standard drink = 10 g of pure alcohol

= 375 ml of beer that is 3.5% abv

= 100 ml of wine

= one nip (30 ml) of spirits

However, glasses used to serve wine may be bigger than the standard size, and many drinks are stronger than this. "Strong" beers are those over 6 percent abv and many wines are 14 percent abv.

How much is safe?

Guidelines for adults vary in different countries, as research into the effects of alcohol is not conclusive. The precise level for any individual depends on body size and how well his or her body metabolizes alcohol.

There has been limited research into levels of alcohol that are safe for young people and children to drink. It is recommended that young people under 16 should not drink any alcohol at all.

Wine glasses in bars and restaurants may hold as much as 8.5 oz (250 ml).

Safe drinking limits

Women should not drink more than 0.6–0.85 oz (16–24 g) of alcohol a day, up to 3.95 oz (112 g) a week. Men should not drink more than about 0.85-1.1 oz (24–32 g) of alcohol a day, up to 5.93 oz (168 g) a week.

Daily limits	Alcohol	U.S. standard drinks	U.K. units	Australia standard drinks
Women	0.6–0.85 oz (16–24 g)	1–1.5	2–3	1.6–2.4
Men	0.85–1.1oz (24–32 g)	1.5–2	3–4	2.4–3.2

2 Alcohol and the body

Alcohol affects the body as soon as someone starts drinking. Some effects wear off once the body has broken down the alcohol. Someone who drinks too much, though, risks serious and lasting harmful effects.

What happens when someone drinks

Within minutes of someone having an alcoholic drink, his or her body begins to absorb alcohol and be affected by it.

An **enzyme** in the stomach called alcohol dehydrogenase (ADH) starts to break down alcohol, but some of the alcohol passes straight through the wall of the stomach and the small intestine into the bloodstream. In the blood, it is carried first to the liver, where another enzyme starts to break it down. The liver can only process an average of about 0.3 oz (8 g) of alcohol each hour.

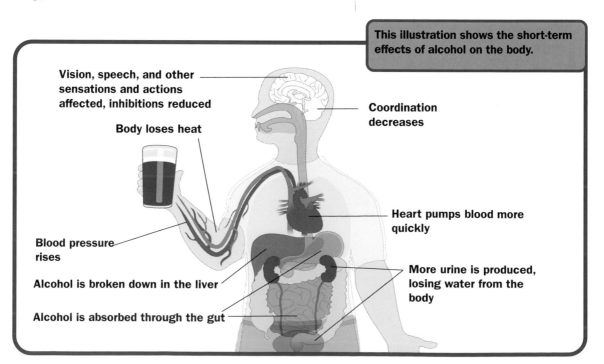

This illustration shows the short-term effects of alcohol on the body.

Vision, speech, and other sensations and actions affected, inhibitions reduced

Body loses heat

Coordination decreases

Blood pressure rises

Heart pumps blood more quickly

Alcohol is broken down in the liver

More urine is produced, losing water from the body

Alcohol is absorbed through the gut

Meanwhile, the blood carries alcohol around the body where it begins to have an effect. Alcohol is a **depressant** and slows down body processes. It relaxes the heart muscles, slowing the heartbeat. It slows the breathing rate, too. The blood vessels expand and more blood flows to the skin, which is why drinking makes people feel warmer and sometimes look flushed. Alcohol also affects the brain and central nervous system. In small amounts, it can make people feel relaxed and uninhibited, but in larger doses it has more serious effects.

Getting drunk

Many people feel the effects of drinking even a small amount of alcohol. When someone drinks more than about 0.3 oz (8 g) of alcohol an hour, the body cannot remove alcohol from the blood quickly enough, and he or she begins to get drunk. Alcohol interferes with the transmission of nerve impulses within the brain. This makes it hard to think straight and slows reaction times. It can also cause blurred vision, uncoordinated movement, and slurred speech, as the nerve impulses to and from other parts of the body are disrupted.

"Just because you're not always out 'getting drunk' don't assume you're drinking at safe levels. Heavy drinkers build up a tolerance. Building tolerance might mean that you don't notice the effects so much, but the fact remains: the more you drink, the greater the risk to your health. If you're building up tolerance, that is a warning sign."

Dr. Michael Wilks, British Medical Association

HEALTH WARNING

It is very important for a woman who is pregnant, or trying to become pregnant, not to drink. Alcohol can harm the unborn baby. Unfortunately, the effects of drinking are most significant in the early weeks of pregnancy when a woman may not even know she is pregnant.

? WHAT COUNTS AS A BINGE?

In the United States, binge drinking is defined as four standard drinks for a woman (1.9 oz/54.4 g) and five for a man (2.4 oz/68 g). However the official definition varies from country to country.

Being sick

Drinking a large quantity in one session—called **binge drinking**—can make someone sick, as alcohol aggravates the lining of the stomach. Regular binge drinking can cause a **stomach ulcer**, which is painful, may bleed, and can be life threatening if untreated. Being sick helps to protect the body, as the alcohol that is vomited cannot harm the body further. But someone who gets to this stage has already drunk far too much.

Passing out

If someone drinks excessively, he or she may lose consciousness. This is very dangerous. An

IT HAPPENED TO ME

I went to a dance with some of my friends, and Elinor was acting a bit odd. After a while, she was swaying and stumbling around, and her eyes were going all over the place. It turned out she'd been drinking before coming out. Then within minutes, she was throwing up. We dragged her to the toilets, but she passed out. We were all so scared. The security guards at the dance called an ambulance, and she had to have her stomach pumped at the hospital.

Olivia, 15

Drinking until being sick or passing out is increasingly common but can be very dangerous.

unconscious person may get sick, breathe in vomit, and suffocate. Never leave alone someone who has passed out after drinking too much. It is vital that the unconscious person is put into the recovery position (see illustration) to reduce the danger of death. In this position, vomit will leak from the mouth and not block the throat. Learning how to put someone in the recovery position could save a friend's life—it's worth putting in a few minutes to practice it.

Anyone who has drunk so much that he or she passes out is at risk of alcohol poisoning (see page 16). If you are with someone who passes out after drinking, make sure that he or she gets to a hospital emergency room—but don't let someone who has been drinking drive the person there.

The morning after

Drinking too much often leads to a hangover the next day. The usual signs of a hangover are a headache, feeling or being sick, diarrhea, and a nasty taste in the mouth. The hangover is caused by acetaldehyde (produced by the liver breaking down alcohol), **dehydration,** and a lack of vital salts in the body. The water and salts have been used up by the body trying to dispose of the alcohol. The only way to get rid of the hangover is to rehydrate the body by drinking nonalcoholic drinks and wait for the acetaldehyde to be broken down.

Putting someone into the recovery position may save a life. In this position the airways are open—the person will not suffocate on vomit or swallow his or her tongue.

1. Kneel beside the person, loosen his or her clothing, and remove any jewelry. Check that the airways are open and that he or she is breathing.

2. Extend and bend the arm at 90 degrees to the body, with the palm upward. Bring the other arm over the person's chest, putting the back of his or her hand against the cheek nearest to you. Raise and bend the top leg. Gently roll the person toward you by pulling on the bent knee.

3. Adjust the top leg so that it is at 90 degrees to the body. Make sure the person's head is resting on his or her hand and the head is sideways, with the mouth angled so that vomit can drain out and the airways are open.

Healthy and alcohol-damaged livers: a fatty liver (left), a scarred and enlarged liver with cirrhosis (center), and a healthy liver (right).

Long-term effects

If the short-term effects of alcohol are unpleasant, the long-term effects are much worse. Drinking too much over a long period can affect a person's physical appearance, mental health, and physical health, and it can lead to **dependency** (alcoholism).

Damage to the body

Drinking hazardous levels of alcohol over an extended period of time can cause serious and sometimes irreversible damage to the body. It can affect the liver, the heart, the brain, and other vital organs. Drinking is also a risk factor in many types of cancer. Every

Will he be able to give up?

Dear Agony Aunt,
My friend's always going out, and he drinks several beers most nights. I've told him he should rein it in a bit in case he becomes an alcoholic, but he just laughs at me and says he can give up easily later so it's not a problem. Is that true?
LeRoy, 17

Dear LeRoy,
You're right to worry about your friend. He may not be dependent on alcohol now, but he could become dependent. Can he have days without drinking, or does that make him jittery or anxious? Even if he's not dependent, he's probably damaging his body by drinking so much. More and more young people are suffering the effects of serious alcohol misuse, so he can't assume it doesn't matter yet. Why not suggest he goes for a checkup? A simple blood test will show whether he has damaged his liver yet, and his doctor will advise him to cut down. The advice will carry more weight coming from a doctor than from you.

year around 22,000 people in the United States and 8,000 people in the United Kingdom die from diseases directly caused by drinking alcohol. In addition, it is a factor in—or the sole cause of—many fatal accidents.

Liver damage

Fatty liver disease happens when fat builds up in the cells of the liver. It can reverse if a person stops drinking, but—as it has no symptoms—many people are unaware they have it. About one in three people with fatty liver disease go on to get alcoholic hepatitis, which is an inflammation of the liver. Mild hepatitis can be discovered only with a blood test, so again many people don't realize they have it. Someone with severe hepatitis feels generally unwell and develops jaundice (a yellow tinge to the skin and whites of the eyes). Very severe hepatitis can lead to liver failure and death.

Cirrhosis is a very serious condition that affects about one in ten people who drink heavily over an extended period. Liver tissue is replaced by scar tissue, which is unable to function like normal liver tissue. The damage is not reversed if someone stops drinking. In cases of severe cirrhosis, a liver transplant might offer the only chance of survival. Anyone with cirrhosis or hepatitis must stop drinking completely. It usually takes 10–20 years to develop cirrhosis—even so, Gary Reinbach, 22, died of cirrhosis in the United Kingdom in 2009 after drinking heavily from the age of 13.

Problem drinkers may be given a second chance by a liver transplant, but only if they are able to give up alcohol.

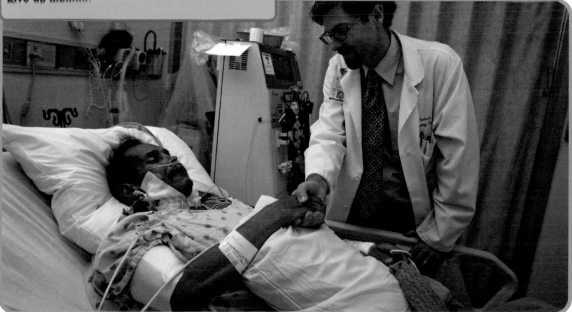

IT HAPPENED TO ME

It was my boyfriend's 21st birthday, and there was a tradition in his college of "drinking your age." He downed 21 shots of vodka. It was more than he could deal with. His friends called me to the hospital, but he never regained consciousness. I saw his mom go in the room. That look she gave me—I couldn't bear to stay there. I left, and he died a couple of hours later.

Angela, 20

Alcohol poisoning

Alcohol poisoning can happen when someone drinks a very large amount of alcohol in one session. The alcohol completely overloads the liver, which is not able to remove it quickly enough. The alcohol then travels in the blood to harm other parts of the body. The heartbeat and breathing can become irregular or stop. In the worst cases, alcohol poisoning can lead to organ failure, brain damage, and death. Even if

Alcohol poisoning is a medical emergency and requires immediate attention. Sadly, ambulance crews are all too used to getting calls like this.

someone with alcohol poisoning is taken to hospital, it may be too late to save him or her.

After someone has stopped drinking, the level of alcohol in the blood may continue to rise, as any drink remaining in the stomach can still be absorbed. The drinker's condition may deteriorate even after losing consciousness, so it is important to put him or her in the recovery position (see page 13) while seeking help. This prevents the drinker choking on vomit, a common cause of death after drinking too much. Other causes of death can be the heart or breathing stopping, or extreme dehydration. Someone who survives alcohol poisoning may suffer permanent brain damage caused by severe dehydration.

The warning signs of alcohol poisoning include confusion, vomiting, seizures (fits), slow or irregular breathing, low body temperature, pale or blue-tinged skin, unresponsiveness or unconsciousness.

"Rates of alcohol-use disorders in adolescence are very high, and adolescents with alcohol-use disorders also experienced elevated rates of drug use disorders and depression as young adults."

Dr. Paul Rohde, PhD, Oregon Research Institute, Eugene, Oregon

BEER BELLIES

The characteristic beer belly many men have is the result of drinking too much, but it is not just the high **caloric** value of alcoholic drinks that causes weight gain. Alcohol prevents the body breaking down fat to use as fuel, so fat builds up in the body. Being overweight has its own health risks, including heart disease and **diabetes**.

Will I become an alcoholic?

Dear Agony Aunt,
My uncle is an alcoholic, and so was my granddad. I didn't know my dad because he died in a car crash when I was a baby. I don't want to upset my mom by asking about it, but I'm worried that he was an alcoholic, too. Does it mean that I'll become an alcoholic if I start to drink?
Anthony, 15

Dear Anthony,
*Many factors affect whether a person is likely to drink too much or become alcohol dependent. Your environment makes a big difference—if alcohol is available and freely used around you, you are more likely to drink. **Genetic** makeup plays only a small part in alcohol misuse. Having close relatives who are alcohol dependent may make you slightly more likely to become dependent yourself. But many people who see the effects of alcohol misuse in the family try hard to avoid the same problems themselves. No one should ever use genetics as an excuse for drinking alcohol; it is always a choice you can make, regardless of your family history.*

Becoming an alcoholic

Someone who misuses alcohol over a long period may become an alcoholic —he or she becomes dependent on alcohol and finds it difficult to function without it. Alcohol dependency is a physical and **psychological** condition. Alcoholics suffer physical **withdrawal symptoms** if they cannot get alcohol, as well as often feeling anxious, desperate, jittery, or aggressive.

The slide into alcohol dependency can be gradual. Many people are dependent on alcohol without realizing it. Most are ordinary people living ordinary lives, perhaps drinking every night but never binge drinking and not aware they are dependent.

Alcohol and mental health

Misusing alcohol over an extended time can lead to mental health problems. It is particularly dangerous in young people, as the brain continues to develop after adolescence, well into the twenties. Alcohol impairs development of the brain, memory function, and learning ability.

Alcohol misuse is linked with increased risk of depression and suicide. Because alcohol is a depressant, it can make any tendency to depression worse. Alcohol changes the chemistry of the brain, increasing the risk of depression. A person already suffering from depression has brain chemistry that takes less of a "push" to begin a depressed episode. Among the strongest risk factors in suicide are depression and misuse of alcohol or other substances.

ALCOHOL, OBESITY, AND DEPRESSION

Women with an alcohol disorder at the age of 24 are more than three times as likely as others to be **obese** at the age of 27. These obese women have a doubled risk of being depressed when they reach 30.

Hitting the bottle when depressed cannot help, and it can make depression worse.

FAQ

3 Why worry?

Is it a problem if some people drink too much? Or is it up to them if they want to drink? Alcohol misuse is not simply a personal issue, no matter what drinkers may say. Excess drinking has repercussions for others—the drinker's friends, family, and wider society.

How does alcohol cause problems?

Misusing alcohol can affect a person's ability to work or study. Alcohol makes it difficult to concentrate and think clearly, and misuse over time damages the brain and affects memory function. Excessive

IT HAPPENED TO ME

I started drinking at 14, going out with friends, just on the weekends. I felt more at ease with people with a few drinks inside me. I made friends, as everyone thought I was cool. I drank more and more, until I was passing out every weekend. Then I started to skip school so I could drink in the afternoon at home when no one was there. I used to do well in school, but by the time I was 16, I was failing every class. Even that didn't stop me from drinking—I just drank more to block out my failures.

It took me a long time to realize what I was doing. I've now been through **rehab,** and I'm living in a **halfway house.**

Helen, 19

Drinking too much may lead to disturbed sleep, resulting in exhaustion and an inability to concentrate, affecting school or college work.

Homeless people often turn to alcohol to dull their pain and desperation; drinking problems are common among people who live on the streets.

drinking can also have an impact on family life and relationships. Drinking too much can lead to arguments, family breakdown, damaged relationships, and abuse within the family. The pressure of living with someone who drinks too much can harm family members and make them ill, too.

Damage is not limited to the drinker and his or her family. Alcohol misuse is related to social problems such as crime, unemployment, and homelessness. It has a financial cost to society. Money from taxes is used to fight alcohol-related crime, to pay benefits to people who cannot work or support their families because of their drinking and, in some countries, it is used to pay health-care costs for people whose drinking has made them ill.

YOUNG PEOPLE DRINKING

- In the United States, more than 8 percent of eighth graders, 16 percent of 15–16-year-olds, and 24 percent of 17–18-year-olds reported in 2009 that they had recently indulged in binge drinking (more than five drinks).

- A survey in 2008 found that 28 percent of girls aged 15–16 in Ireland had been drunk in the last month.

- In Australia, around a quarter of 12–15-year-olds say they drink alcohol at least sometimes.

> "Research indicates that most binge drinkers are ordinary teenagers from ordinary backgrounds, and increasingly it is young girls who are placing themselves at risk—and that risk is very high indeed. Risky alcohol consumption contributes to a significant amount of teenage injury including falls, drownings, assaults, and of course, car accidents. It is also a major factor in teenage suicide."
>
> **Wendy Loxley, National Drug Research Institute, Curtin University of Technology, Perth, Australia**

About 5,000 young people under 21 die every year in the United States as a result of car crashes, murders, and suicides linked to drinking.

IT HAPPENED TO ME

I'd been going out with Owen for a few weeks, and I wasn't planning to have sex with him. We went to a party, and then with some friends we went to a park on the way home and drank more. I think we had sex in some bushes, but I don't remember very clearly. Because I wasn't planning sex, I didn't have any protection. When I found out five weeks later I was pregnant, I was horrified. I'd already stopped seeing Owen, so I was totally alone.

Krystal, 18

Risky behavior

Someone who is drunk may make foolish choices because alcohol impairs judgment. The person might take risks he or she would not take when sober, such as performing dangerous stunts or dares, taking other drugs, or having unsafe sex.

It's not just about taking risks. Alcohol reduces reaction times and physical coordination, so even activities that would normally be safe can be dangerous. In the United States, 20–40 percent of accident and emergency admissions are related to drinking, and at nighttime this rises to 80 percent.

Damaged relationships

Persistent drinking can damage family relationships. People sometimes lose their jobs, homes, families, and friends as a result of heavy drinking.

It is very stressful living with a problem drinker. The person may act irrationally or aggressively when he or she wants a drink or is drunk. It can cause serious family problems if the drinker spends a lot of money; is often out drinking; or loses interest in work, family, and friends. The parents of a young drinker may tell him or her to leave home. The partner of an adult drinker may leave or throw the drinker out.

Children suffer particularly badly when a parent misuses alcohol. Children cannot easily leave and live somewhere else, though some run away to escape the daily pressure of life with an alcoholic parent. This can be very dangerous—some end up living on the streets and even turning to alcohol themselves.

Arguments, neglect, and abuse are just some of the issues facing children and young people who live in a family affected by alcohol misuse.

"There is a direct link between the increasing violence and alcohol consumption. If we increase the cost of alcohol, then it is less likely that young people will be able to obtain it."

Nahum Itzkovitz, Welfare and Social Services Ministry, Israel

Money troubles

Alcohol is expensive, and people who drink a lot often overspend. That might sound like a trivial problem, but it can lead to real hardship or to crime. Lack of money is very stressful for the family of a drinker; seeing money that is needed for clothes, food, or bills being wasted on drink is very traumatic for the rest of the family.

Alcohol and crime

There is a strong link between drinking and criminal activity. When people are drunk, they are less able

Alcohol can fuel arguments and make people aggressive.

to consider their actions and more likely to do something that they would never do when sober. They might act violently, become argumentative and get into a fight, or feel they are invincible and can ignore laws designed to keep people safe.

Antisocial behavior

Sometimes, people with an alcohol problem steal in order to get money to spend on alcohol. People who have been drinking may cause a public nuisance. They may vandalize property, be sick or urinate in doorways and streets, leave bottles and cans in parks and other public places, make a lot of noise, or pick fights with passersby. This behavior makes the environment unpleasant for other people. It can be quite scary, too, having to walk past a group of drunk, rowdy people.

Under the influence of alcohol, people may vandalize property and carry out other crimes that they would never consider when sober.

Should we kick my brother out?

Dear Agony Aunt,
My dad is threatening to throw my brother, Tyler, out of the house. Tyler's been drinking since he was 14 (he's now 17), and it's just completely out of hand. I know that he steals stuff from our dad and sells it to buy drink. It's awful when he's here, but he's my brother, and I don't want to lose him. Is it fair to kick him out? Can't we help him?
Callum, 14

Dear Callum,
It must be very hard for you both to live with Tyler's drinking. Perhaps your dad hopes that a "wake-up call" could get Tyler to change. Try to persuade your dad to get in touch with your local alcohol problem service and ask what support is available for your family. They can help Tyler cut back his drinking and look at why he is drinking so much. Perhaps Tyler could see his doctor, too, to check whether there is an underlying problem, such as depression, which is leading to his drinking. If you can't persuade your dad to do this first, he needs to find out where Tyler plans to go when he leaves home. Will he be staying with friends? If he has nowhere to go, living on the streets is likely to make his problems worse, so perhaps your dad could find a place in a hostel for Tyler.

HEALTH WARNING

Someone who is drunk can't sober up quickly by drinking black coffee, taking a cold shower, or going for a brisk walk. Even if the person feels more alert afterward, the amount of alcohol in his or her system will not have reduced. The only way to sober up is to wait while the body processes the alcohol.

Drinking and driving

One of the most common and dangerous crimes related to alcohol is drinking and driving. Most countries set a legal limit on the amount of alcohol a person may have in his or her blood and still drive, but even driving with alcohol levels below the legal limit is dangerous. If someone is going to drive, it's best if he or she doesn't drink at all. Around one in six of all deaths on the road involve a drunk driver. Often, people are still over the limit for driving the morning after a drinking session.

The impact of law breaking

The immediate victims of crime are not the only ones to suffer from alcohol-related crime. A young person who has uncharacteristically committed a crime when drunk may suffer for years as a result. This might include losing his or her driving license, job, college place, valued relationship, or freedom.

Someone stopped for suspected drunk-driving, or involved in a road accident, is likely to be breath-tested by police. The Breathalyzer detects alcohol in the breath and may be followed up by a blood test.

There may be restrictions on travel to places he or she wants to visit, and many career choices may be closed if a young person has a criminal record. The person's family will be distressed and may suffer abuse from other people, or financial hardship, especially if the drinker is fined or imprisoned.

The cost of alcohol misuse

Paying for the damage done by drinkers costs money. Funds spent on fixing damage, and on pursuing and punishing drunken criminals cannot be spent on other social benefits. Public money is used to care for people with alcohol problems and give financial support to their families. The work time lost to alcohol-related illness is a cost carried by employers and also by society as a whole. People who are not earning are not paying taxes or contributing to the economy, so everyone else has to make up for them.

A LEGAL DRINKING AGE

Many countries have laws to stop young people from drinking. In most countries that have an age limit, it is 18. In the United States, people under 21 may not buy or drink alcohol. In the United Kingdom, anyone over 18 may buy alcohol, and people over 16 may drink some types of alcohol with a meal in a restaurant. In some Muslim countries, drinking is illegal for people of any age. Travelers should check the local laws.

Anyone suspected of driving after drinking too much may be stopped and arrested and could face a fine, driving ban, or imprisonment.

FAQ

4 Why do people drink?

People drink for many reasons. The situations in which they drink and the drinks they choose are also varied.

Social drinking

Many people drink to help them relax and to enjoy social occasions more, and because they like the taste of alcoholic drinks. For adults, moderate drinking for this reason is usually not harmful and may be part of having a good time.

Some young people drink because they want to be like everyone else— their friends are drinking, and they want to part of the crowd. Or they

IT HAPPENED TO ME

By the age of 16, most of my friends were drinking every weekend. I'm Muslim, and I'm not allowed to drink, but I didn't want to anyway. It was quite frightening to see some of the things my friends did when they were drunk. After a while, they stopped hassling me to drink. Then when I got a driver's license, I could drive them around to parties, and they were quite happy I didn't drink.

Tehmina, 17

Moderate drinking is an enjoyable and safe part of social occasions for many adults.

People can have just as much fun with friends if they do not drink alcohol.

might drink because they think it looks cool or grown-up, or even because it is forbidden and so feels rebellious or daring. These are less-good reasons. Indeed, it is more grown-up to be independent and make your own choices, so if you don't want to drink, stick by your decision. Often, other people are too caught up in their own activity to notice or care whether everyone is drinking.

Drinking to get drunk

Some people like the feeling of being drunk—either being a little tipsy or getting completely drunk. Binge drinking or going on a "bender" involves drinking dangerous amounts of alcohol. People who routinely drink a lot may, after a while, drink just because they have become accustomed to and dependent on alcohol and are no longer thinking about whether or not to drink.

"If you start drinking before 14 years of age, you double the risk of alcohol dependence at age 21."

John Toumbourou, Professor of Health Psychology, Deakin University, Australia

TEEN DRINKERS

A 2007 report in the U.S. found that, among other causes, teens who have a strong desire for new experiences and sensations are more likely to use alcohol than others in their peer group.

HEALTH WARNING

If you or someone you know is tempted to drink to escape misery or problems, look for a better solution. Getting help from a professional counselor or doctor to deal with the underlying problems is a productive way forward, but drinking is not. Alcohol cannot make things better and can often make things much worse.

Drinking to forget

Sometimes, people drink to forget their problems or the harsh reality of their lives. This is a sad situation in which alcohol becomes a crutch, and it can quickly lead to alcohol dependence. As alcohol is a depressant, it is not a solution to depression—it can only make things worse.

Friends and family

Seeing alcohol used around you sets mental patterns of what you consider "normal." If you see parents and other adult family members drinking moderately, not drinking inappropriately, you are more likely to use alcohol sensibly yourself when you grow up. If you see people misusing alcohol, you are more likely to follow the same path—unless you make an effort not to do so.

If children see irresponsible alcohol use around them, they are more likely to misuse alcohol themselves when they grow up.

Seeing parents enjoying social activities without alcohol will make children less likely to rely on alcohol in social situations when they are older.

IT HAPPENED TO ME

My parents always drank quite a lot and let me have sips of alcohol. I had my first full drink when I was 13, and after that it quickly got out of hand. I'd start with breezers and cruisers. They taste nice and you can drink lots of them. I'd have about 12, then move on to **bourbon** and vodka. I could drink a bottle of each… I've had blackouts, which is scary. I'd be talking to friends and they'd say I'd done something crazy the night before and I'd have no idea what they were talking about. They once said I'd had sex with a guy I don't know. I panicked and went to the clinic for a check-up. Luckily I hadn't caught anything but waiting for the results was so scary. I try not to drink so much now. I never want to go through that again.

Cassie, 16

If you spend a lot of time with friends who drink, or go to a lot of events where alcohol is available and freely consumed, you are more likely to develop a habit of drinking alcohol than if you spend most of your leisure time in alcohol-free environments. People often act to fit in with others without even being aware that they are doing it.

The availability of alcohol also influences how much someone is likely to drink. For this reason, the law tries to make it difficult for young people under the legal drinking age to buy or get hold of alcohol.

FAQ

5 Time to party?

Many people drink alcohol at social events—at parties, in clubs, bars, and restaurants. Relaxing with friends is fun, but to remain safe, it's important to be careful, especially around people you don't know, whether or not you choose to drink.

What young people drink

Young people often drink beer, because it is cheap. Some young people drink **flavored malt beverages**. These are sweet drinks, often with a fruity flavor that masks the taste of the alcohol. It's easy to drink too many because they don't taste of alcohol.

I don't want to drink, but...

Dear Agony Aunt,
I like going out with my friends, but they say I'll have more fun partying if I drink. I don't really want to drink, but I don't want to be left out either. How can I tell them it's not for me? Or should I just have one or two drinks to keep them quiet?
Kris, 18

Dear Kris,
You really don't have to drink if you don't want to. If they are real friends, they will not give you up just because you don't drink. Tell them you have a great time with them anyway and don't need alcohol to enjoy yourself. You can remind them it's good having a sober friend in the group—you can help out if anything goes wrong, and you can drive people home safely.

Some young people drink spirits, such as vodka or gin, often mixed with fruit juice or fizzy drinks. Boys (more often than girls) may drink large volumes of beer.

Mixed drinks

For parties, people might make a fruit punch. This is a large bowl of drink, made by mixing different alcoholic drinks and fruit juices together. Once the party has been going for a while, the original recipe may be forgotten as people pour in random bottles. It can be very difficult to tell how alcoholic a drink like this is, and how to pace drinking it sensibly. For anyone who is going to drink, it's best to avoid mixed drinks like this and only drink from identifiable bottles or cans.

"Spiked" drinks

Occasionally, someone will "spike" another person's drink, adding extra alcohol without his or her knowledge. This is very dangerous. The person who does it might think it's just a laugh, trying to get someone drunk so that he or she looks foolish. But someone who has had alcohol without realizing it may be in danger as a result. They are at risk of alcohol poisoning, driving over the limit, or doing something risky. Some people spike drinks **maliciously**, not for a laugh but because they want to take advantage of the drinker—this could include sexual assault or rape.

It is easy for someone to add more alcohol to a fruit cup or punch without other drinkers noticing, making this a risky choice of drink at a party.

HEALTH WARNING

If you are drinking in a public place or with people you don't know—even if you have chosen a soft drink—don't let your drink out of your sight. Don't let someone you don't know well or trust buy a drink for you when you can't see or hear what he or she is getting. Many bars, especially student bars, sell "spike detectors" which you can use to test whether your drink has been spiked.

A drink left on a table in a crowded club could easily be spiked with more alcohol or a drug while its owner is not looking.

Drink and drugs

While drinking too much alcohol is dangerous in itself, mixing alcohol with other drugs can be especially dangerous. The heartbeat or breathing rate of someone who takes another depressant drug can drop to critically low levels. Depressant drugs include **heroin**, **codeine**-based painkillers, and **valium**. There is a high risk of overdose if someone takes these with alcohol since the alcohol contributes to their depressant effect. Taking alcohol with a stimulant drug means that the body is struggling to cope with drugs that are trying to do different things at the same time. Stimulants include **cocaine** and **speed** (amphetamines).

Are medicines OK?

Drugs are not just illegal street drugs like cocaine and **marijuana**. They include medicines that you can buy over the counter or take on prescription. These, too, can interact with alcohol to give dangerous results. A person who is taking any medication, even something like cough medicine, a cold remedy, a painkiller, or herbal remedies, should never drink unless a doctor has said that the drugs are safe to use with alcohol.

HEALTH WARNING

It's very dangerous to drink and take **paracetamol**, so someone who has taken a paracetamol tablet or a cold remedy containing paracetamol should not drink any alcohol at all. Paracetamol and alcohol both put a strain on the liver; it's easy to cause liver damage by mixing the two, even if the amount of alcohol on its own would not have been a problem.

FAQ

6 Can people drink safely?

Some things are bad for your body however little you do them—smoking is one example. But alcohol is not always bad for the body. It is possible for adults to drink within safe limits and enjoy drinking without risk. Indeed, small amounts of alcohol may even bring some health benefits for many people.

Does my mom have a drinking problem?

Dear Agony Aunt,
My mom drinks a glass of wine every evening. She rarely has more than one glass, but it is nearly every day. Should I be worried about her?
Amy, 14

Dear Amy,
It sounds as though your mom is enjoying a drink sensibly. If she is only drinking a glass a day, and it is not a very large glass, she is drinking within safe limits for an adult woman, and you don't need to worry about her. Your mom may even benefit from her glass of wine. Research shows that, for adults, one unit of alcohol a day reduces the risk of heart disease.

A good drink?

Scientific research suggests that drinking some alcohol is actually good for adults. Teetotallers (people who drink no alcohol at all) have higher rates of heart disease than people who drink moderately. Moderate drinking can be good for mental and emotional health, too.

Research has found that, for adults, one or two units of alcohol a day can provide some protection against heart disease and blockages in the arteries. At the same time, though, any alcohol raises the risk of some types of cancer, and drinking too much wipes out all health benefits.

> "Responsible drinking may actually prevent the common diseases of old age. The mortality rate [among moderate drinkers] is 20 percent lower, and the rate of heart disease 40 percent lower than in **abstainers** with similar behavior and [physical]characteristics."
>
> Dr. R. Curtis Ellison, Professor of Medicine and Public Health at Boston University School of Medicine, Boston, MA

Alcoholic drink forms a part of many social events and rituals, and many experts believe that in small amounts it is good for most adults.

Alcohol and head injuries

A study in 2006 found that people who had drunk low amounts of alcohol and then suffered a head injury were 24 percent less likely to die than those who had taken no alcohol; people who had drunk a lot were 73 percent more likely to die of their head injury. A recent report involving multiple nations, showed that alcohol is involved in 30 percent of adult hospital admissions.

It can be difficult for people to keep track of their drinking if a waiter or host tops off the glass.

Sensible drinking

Adults who want to enjoy moderate drinking can do so by pacing their alcohol consumption and following simple guidelines.

Eating something before drinking will slow the rate at which alcohol passes through the wall of the stomach and intestine into the bloodstream. Another way of reducing the impact of alcohol is to alternate alcoholic and nonalcoholic drinks. Always having a glass of water on hand and taking sips every now and then means that the concentration of alcohol in the gut is reduced, too. It's important for each person to drink at the pace that suits him or her. As everyone's body is different, it is foolish to try to keep pace with other people, matching them drink for drink.

Not all at once

The safe limits for drinking alcohol, stated in standard drinks or units of alcohol, are broken into a daily maximum and a weekly maximum. It is not safe to use all the week's allowance in one or two big drinking sessions. A little alcohol taken frequently is safer for the body than the same total amount of alcohol taken all at once.

Take control

It's difficult to keep control of alcohol consumption if someone else is filling the glass all the time. Someone who allows his or her glass to be topped off before it is empty will quickly lose track of how much he or she has drunk. It's all right to leave unfinished drink in a glass, just as it's all right to leave unfinished food on a plate, and better than feeling unwell after drinking or eating too much.

Anyone who is going out and intends to drink needs to plan beforehand how he or she will get home. This could include getting a lift with someone who is not drinking, booking a taxi, or finding out the times of public transportation. It is dangerous to drink and then drive or cycle.

It can be deadly to mix drink with drugs of any other kind. Anyone who has already taken drugs of any type should refuse alcoholic drinks.

Anyone who is going to an event where he or she will drink should make sure there is a designated driver who is not drinking, or another safe way of getting home.

DANGEROUS CYCLING

A United States study found that having a blood-alcohol level at or above the legal limit for driving led to a 2,000 percent increase in the risk of death or serious injury among cyclists.

7 Getting help

If you know someone who has an alcohol problem, or if you have an alcohol problem yourself, there is plenty of help available to sort it out. No one has to struggle alone with a drinking problem.

I think I've got a drinking problem

Dear Agony Aunt,
I have been drinking regularly since I was 14, and I think my drinking is out of hand. I spend all my money on alcohol, and I'm drunk three or four nights a week. The nights I'm not drinking, I can't think of anything to do with myself. How can I get help without getting into trouble?
Darren, 16

Dear Darren,
You have taken the important first step in recognizing you have a problem and wanting to tackle it, so well done. Your first stop should be your doctor or a counselor at school. They won't tell your parents or the police—you won't get into trouble, and your treatment will be confidential. They will help you assess how much you actually drink and which situations encourage you to drink. This knowledge will help you build a strategy for reducing your drinking. You might like to contact an organization such as Alcoholics Anonymous or the Samaritans, or your doctor may put you in touch with a local support group. You don't need to do it alone.

Help!

If you need advice about how to help someone with a drinking problem or deal with your own drinking, there are many places you can go. Your family doctor or a school or college doctor or nurse will be able to give advice and run physical tests to see if there is some damage to your body already. There are plenty of support groups and counseling services available for people with a drinking problem. Some of these, such as Alcoholics Anonymous, follow strict 12-step programs, and some are less structured. There are special programs for people under the legal drinking age, too.

Counseling and support services help people who misuse alcohol to explore their problems in a supported environment. There will be a chance to talk about the effects and possible causes and to investigate solutions and coping strategies. In a support group, several people with the same or a similar problem work together under the guidance of one or more trained leaders. In a counseling session, an individual works with a counselor or therapist to investigate and try to solve his or her own problems. Nobody should be afraid to ask for help—there is a form of support to suit everyone.

For someone with a drinking problem, a sympathetic counselor can be an enormous help.

Living with a drinker

Many young people suffer from the effects of living with someone who drinks. It might be a parent, step-parent or older sibling—it can have a terrible effect on your own life.

Never blame yourself for someone else's drinking and don't let the drinker blame you. Each drinker is responsible for his or her own choices. Never believe someone who says your bad behavior (or anything else you have done) has "driven them to drink." It just isn't true.

When one person in a family has a problem with alcohol, the other members of the family often suffer as well.

The loving support of friends and family can help someone with an alcohol problem to seek help and to begin to change his or her behavior.

Look after yourself

A drinking parent might leave the house in a mess, fail to cook meals, or be absent for long periods. There may be too little money to live comfortably; you may witness violence, arguments, and bouts of depression; you or other family members may be shouted at, abused, or even hit. If someone is mistreating you like this, you must ask a trusted adult to intervene. You can ask a teacher, doctor, religious leader, or family friend to help you.

Can I stop them?

You can't force someone else to stop drinking if he or she doesn't want to stop. If you try to encourage the person to seek help and he or she refuses, you need to concentrate instead on making sure that you are safe and that you have the support you need to stop the drinking from having too great an impact on your own life. It is difficult, and you may feel as though you are turning your back on the person—but there are people to help you and —when he or she is ready—the drinker, too.

DRUGS AGAINST ALCOHOL

A doctor might prescribe medicine called Antabuse to help with a drinking problem. This prevents the body from breaking down the alcohol fully, producing unpleasant side effects after a single drink.

Glossary

abstainer someone who does not drink alcohol

bender an extended drinking session

binge drinking drinking a large amount of alcohol in one session

bourbon an American whiskey made from corn

caloric relating to calories, the measure of energy from food or drink

cocaine a drug made from the coca bush

codeine a medicinal drug made from opium poppies; it has a calming, sedative effect

dehydration the removal of water

dependency the state of being reliant on a substance in order to feel happy or even to function normally

depressant something that lowers the heart rate and breathing, and suppresses other bodily functions

diabetes a condition in which the body is unable to regulate the level of sugar in the blood

enzyme a protein that performs a biochemical function in the body

ethanol pure alcohol, C_2H_5OH

fermentation the process of making alcohol from sugar by the action of yeast

flavored malt beverage a sweet-tasting alcoholic drink

genetic relating to genes and the inheritance of properties from one generation to the next

halfway house a place of safe, residential care where people with substance abuse problems may go in between a hospital or rehab center stay and a return to the community

heroin a drug made from sap extracted from the seeds of the opium poppy

maliciously with deliberate bad intentions

marijuana the leaves or resin of the cannabis plant, often smoked as a drug

metabolize to break down and process or absorb

obese very overweight, having a body mass index (calculated by weight in pounds divided by height in inches squared, multiplied by 703) of 30 or more

paracetamol a painkilling drug often used to treat headaches and other minor ailments

psychological relating to the mind

rehab rehabilitation: cleansing the body of misused substances and learning to live without them

shot a measure of alcohol used to serve spirits

speed street name for amphetamines, which stimulate the central nervous system, increasing energy and wakefulness

spike to add alcohol to someone's drink without his or her knowledge

stomach ulcer an area of the stomach that has been damaged by the gastric acid produced to aid digestion, often following irritation from another cause

valium a sedative drug used to treat anxiety, insomnia, seizures, and some other conditions

withdrawal symptoms physical and psychological problems that result from suddenly stopping drinking or using another addictive substance

Further information

WEBSITES

www.aa.org/
Alcoholics Anonymous site offers help with giving up alcohol or living with an alcoholic relative.

www.thecoolspot.gov/
Advice about avoiding alcohol misuse and dealing with peer pressure to drink.

www.familydoctor.org/
Lots of information about health-related issues. Under the "Parents & Kids" tab, special sections for teens, kids, and parents offer a variety of resources.

http://kidshealth.org/teen/
Advice for teens on dealing with all sorts of health-related issues, including alcohol-related matters. The site includes a great section for younger kids, too.

BOOKS

David Aretha, *On the Rocks: Teens and Alcohol*, Children's Press, 2006

Sean Connolly, *Alcohol* (Straight Talking About...), Franklin Watts, 2008

Natasha Friend, *Lush*, Scholastic, Inc., 2007

KidsPeace, *I Have This Friend. . .* , edited by Anna Radev, Hazelden Publishing, 2007

Jillian Powell and John G. Smanich, *Alcohol and Drug Abuse*, Gareth Stevens Publishing, 2008

Index